The Publishers

Red Deer College Press

56 Avenue & 32 Street Box 5005

Red Deer Alberta Canada T4N 5H5

Credits

Cover & Text Design: Charles Cousins

Author Photo: André Jodoin

Printed & Bound in Canada by Best Gagné Printing Ltée
for Red Deer College Press

Acknowledgements

Absinthe, Barscheit, Camrose Review, Canadian Literature, Capilano Review, Edmonton Bullet,
Jorge Frascara, Line, Massachusetts Review, Measurements: Out from Buffalo, Peter Bartl,
Poetry Canada Review, pomflit, Prairie Fire, Prism International, Screens and Tasted Parallels,
Secrets from the Orange Couch, So Far (Talonbooks), Somewhere Across the Border, Temblor,
TransLit, Tyuonyi, West Coast Line, Words We Call Home, Zest

The publishers gratefully acknowledge the financial contribution
of the Alberta Foundation for the Arts, Alberta Culture and
Multiculturalism and The Canada Council.

Canadian Cataloguing in Publication Data

Fred Wah, 1939–

Alley Alley Home Free

(Writing West)

Poems.

ISBN 0-88995-088-1

I.Title. II.Series.

PS8545.A28A74 1992 C811'.54 C92-091352-0

PR9199.3.W35A74 1992

Alley Alley

HOME FREE

FRED WAH

for beep

RED DEER COLLEGE PRESS

To say: "I don't undertand what this means," is, at
least, to recognize that "this" means. The problem is that
meaning is not a totality of sameness and predictability.
Within each word, each sentence, meaning has slipped a
little out of sight and all we have are traces, shadows, still
warm ashes. The meaning available from language goes
beyond the actual instance of this word, that word. A text
is a place where a labyrinth of continually revealing
meanings are available, a place that offers more possibility
than we can be sure we know, sometimes more than we
want to know. It isn't a container, static and apparent.
Rather, it is noisy, frequently illegible. Reading into
meaning starts with a questioning glance, a seemingly
obvious doubloon on a mast. The multiplicity can be read,
should be read, even performed. But then again, perhaps
meaning is intransitive and unreadable, only meant to be
made. No sooner do we name meaning than it dissipates.
As a sure thing, it eludes us. It arouses us to attempt an
understanding, to interpret. But this is usually unsatisfying
since whatever direction we approach from only leads us
to suspect there is no one direction. No single meaning is
the right one because no "right ones" stand still long
enough to get caught. But because we do not know does
not mean we are lost. Something that is strangely familiar,
not quite what we expect, but familiar, is present. That
quick little gasp in the daydream, a sudden sigh of
recognition, a little sock of baby breath. Writing into
meaning starts at the white page, nothing but intention.
This initial blinding clarity needs to be disrupted before
we're tricked into settling for a staged and diluted
paradigm of the "real," the good old familiar, inherited,
understandable, unmistakable lucidity of phrase that feels

safe and sure, a simple sentence, just-like-the-last-time-sentence. One makes (the) difference. Meaning generates and amplifies itself, beyond itself, but never forgets; fragments of its memory and its potency exceed itself with meaning full of desire and can only be found hiding between the words and lines and in a margin large enough for further thought, music at the heart of thinking, go ahead.

"ɛ" not quite there in Delphi's mind slope except for the eggplant but on the périphérique the traffic is something else not unlike the quick movement of the small bug attracted to the light at the edges of the papers under the desk lamp. Now it's raining, finally, after three weeks of heat. Moths and what we call cedar bugs get in their last licks. Hermes comes into the room as a stunned silence in the middle of the yak-yak din, a borderline coyote too excited by the lushness of the minutiae to pee on the post. This means time and space don't really matter. viz. Canada, Cambodia, Canaan, et al.

Called "fat bits" and it breaks up size into the labyrinth. Goes inside the larger to really show the invisibility of the city as only virtual; what remains are real streets and buildings. According to Homer this change in the condition of experience corresponds to Blake's beach. Heaven. Sand. Could this be the shouldering of the world? The specific seems to operate in this, as you say, abandoned way. But to have daughters makes me wish, naturally, for the right kind of jar, like the sack of winds Aeolus gave to Odysseus. Gingerly.

Pausanias is the traveller but yr the journeyer and maybe that's why you cry at night for love. Compadres of the open road. Purest nakedness. Purest silence. Kerenyi says "The gorges over which [you might pass] can be the abysses of unbelievable love affairs..." Not to mention the deep valleys carved out by the rapids of the Selemnus river, which these days is avoided by even the tourists. Some path of sighing and the sacred, some f-stop towards (or away from) memory. Or did you forget you tied your sandals with a double knot?

Maybe the reverse is just the reflective ritualing of the prop, old twin-twisted kerykeion to be leaned on. Any way think of the Chinese dog days and how hot health can get under this hound of heaven. Also, you'd probably get that mirror effect walking up the hill straight from Pausanias' "scattered Greece under Roman rule" simply because the Romans omitted the phoneme schwa or diluted it. Thus the Socrates ticket as a lasting embrace of those pine thickets on that shaped walk up the hillside could only mean the sacred fork or dish used to lift the lonely bull and later fish.

But Hermes really didn't give a shit as the patron of lottery looted the Apolline bank and simply rattled the mantic dice not very apropos that lump of marble lint plopped there on that hillside to convince us of the right answers to our questions yet I've noticed how the wrong ones hang around to stress the absolute equality of real unknowing the late afternoon air and the dust settling onto Delphi's trees and cafes stills the spring cool and refreshing to the tongue thoughts seemed silent feathered and those birds (could they be crows) overhead looked harmless in the light of such hillsides now who can fall or get flung over the cliff for.

Horizon full red w/ a few clouds across the sky down to the river below Sentinel the dream gets dreary mist downstream the dam gathers up huge hackels into the air these freezing nights with the frost for the fog banks slunk against the tree-line each morning's memory of night travel and meeting place in the ditch grass what voice Plato thought dangered the elliptical island now that all this milk Simpson paddled past simply for the pay-off Fenellosa said wasn't there that's what autumn is this year.

Intent • bullet helps the daily postal cut through confusion another language wing strut to world gauge reconstrue type to lip which exits though body shuns the emic enterprise in opposition a little minute particular on the surface of the stone THE at the masthead even the winter-bird hovers beside the truth of itself in a dialect of heat almost fusion this isness a nebula of a dense self-reflected frame that questions limit so everything else north of especially not nation recovers an afternoon life of its own writing through the punct.

Earth seems comfortably familiar and sometimes strangely familial so deja vu green but when it becomes unfamiliar or downtown centre decentral displaced place of all things negative capability a positive incapacity to not know knowing narrates not just Wordsworth's big something else that is determines the rainbow of silence and noise with a clear distortion at the edges of the supratactic acoustics at one end and cosmology at the other underneath dichten condensare's ambiguous ochre dysfunction fragmented rotten Rockies decidedly what's called fear of the hatchtop or self-departure mountain arrived and derived alter-native this making strange still oddly tied to wobbling terra firma no matter what.

Music here like the foot and door quick check of the imprint assuring story construction and that unquestioning privilege of narrative as knowing the only fiction seeming to be the reader everything else counted for or lost only momentarily in the cacophony of murmured concern that is itself distorted by a comfortable pre-text almost uncannily like the Spaniard's view of the new world old habits and all so scenario is not so much a truth like metaphor but only the afterbirth what happens later serves to trample the building debris after treading the winepress alone entwined by the promise of riddles and certain chronicles just for fun since the novel is supposedly only a space project time'll have to launch the rockets of textuary running the line so that a useful physics gets applied to the physiology here literally heat and its measurement but I don't mean the body's natural energeic plot but more a form of ritual or what becomes speech loaded and violent corresponding to such sad things as Virgil's wolf in the fold and the anger of Amarylis nothing of which counts in the predicates of the ontology of anger even this irritating gabble at the edge of the page book takes over from the horizon not as a refusal of silence indeed but then not to neglect the echo either have you ever seen a space not occupied by some sort of grammar the point here to hyphen promise so that you recognize other events as more immediate targets but that's prose for you always hanging around to identify the self what a Quebec poet calls these eternal calculations. that's what I want also the page running and stars of intonation like swimming along the ladder since anger has this prototype that includes retribution I'd suggest cancelling the order and simply leaving the discontinuous as mothers and fathers period being written like that isn't so bad but even so imagine the possibility of literal language-life a

kind of narrative civilization that could tatoo for itself itself
and read only the past tense because in fact that's the only
hay to cut unless you'd rather consider picturing someone
elses lost garden I must admit I've thought of everything as
edible vibration for the pharynx and that's one of those things
you've got to judge prior to recollection if the essential tools
are borrowed off the bench how can we mend our own soul
or is this only frivolous ongoing law as unself-conscious of
dénouement as poor assaulted reader of this facade used
here simply to return you to a resonance of recognition
much like a boring Ontario horizon replaces your attention
with notions of elsewhere but what are you going to do is
fact fiction or are they both strangers to music which is as
much space as time by the way sound articulates distances
and fields and not only pace to verify the solo variant of
course to mobilize subject do we need story but not as the
cruelty of logic and the ultimate "game" only to tell trace and
the range of passions that cause that inmost core to
reverberate actually shake the model up and kick past the
door if we are right our map has considerable light for the
labyrinth my daughters are the kind of immediate people I'm
thinking of who would never scoff a feast or possibly the goal
isn't worth it diction moments usually bring new weather and
all of us possess a lot of randomness so why not confront this
stuttering then let the floods flash but first find out if we're
on to gesture and try not to let it signify ceremony but
housework that hum to the inner ear fragmented into short
songs of plotless therefore dreary life immitating a wandering
or dreaming mind whatever the mode ex out those long
moments from the future as if we knew why we choose any
route but the one home except to think we are already there
the slowest being the quickest though sometimes someone

comes in with news of the others this emotional torture gets to be a bit vast if you let it take over as a mass synapse a little growing awareness of stride will get the smack in the door out.

Thought knot genetic still associational tri-partite basic relations as in microlinguistic BU BR and BS as Duncan pointed out through HD Schrödinger grew crystal eyes for the multiple yet maybe the whole chromosome fibre an aperiodic solid this movement no net or labyrinth Tisserande's body enclosed within the stars as clues that's all we have this encyclopaediatic devotion to system woven codes of straight desire not thread as a guaranteed familiarity to pluck further prehension from the raven/magpie bridge but as Jake says in *Feathers to Iron* not her epiphany because it has moved on and you must do likewise simply to keep up (with her).

I'd thought he'd riprapped that wall of the page or my mind with mountains creeks trees and gravel years ago.

But then stone art pebbled the lichen with possible nouns.

Later story as an historical event cartooned itself; I played a cloud of thought or talk.

Where to go to get the word rubble now or as you say fair producing sky weather may eventually.

MUSIC AT THE HEART OF THINKING EIGHTY-SOMETHING
(after Christine Stewart)

Yesterday in Chinatown I bought gai lan seeds. Chinese brocolli. The green, crunchy stalks, blanched, and ladled over with oyster sauce, make a fine lunch w/ rice, maybe some barbecued duck. This morning in my daughter's kitchen in Vancouver I think of you and the gai lan. The connection isn't my choice; to me, your skin has always showed a flush, a quizzical pudeur. Will thought forever credit nonsense and the exact measure of our hunger and what about our fever?

MUSIC AT THE HEART OF THINKING EIGHTY
(for Bill Sylvester)

Why then the one whirlpool when all the container
two leaks depth through its seams splendour
soaks the sands sprung three as song and not desire
for the polar axle gravity gave no chance for four
his meta(m) five outstripped his harrowing death
lyric left over from six both but let him —
us who want to be enduring messengers seven will
so said the wept-for fountain's Lament
only nine imagined water seeps from the mountainside
maybe that's why we wait or spring's beach butterfly's
touch informs new distances yet another story zinging
motive you and your bike's antennae spanned earth
but the words all over the edge thirteen taste comes
thirsty

MUSIC AT THE HEART OF THINKING EIGHTY-ONE
(for Karl Siegler)

Sometimes all it is is a simple interpolation not so falsely from the laws of narrative since you don't name her her perfumed head imaged quickly adolescent freedom and all possibility including everything to drink but maybe reading her she's my girl this pursuit meant to include marriage as soon as possible car job house who'd have thought smell could linger in lingo or car tires whisper the light that night right in front of all the happinesses prior to life and death love's same old story could be that's when meaning starts.

MUSIC AT THE HEART OF THINKING EIGHTY-TWO
(for Bill Robertson)

When I saw the angels movie
where we get to hear all that thinking out
loud speaking as Friday night theatre aire
(Writing more mass, maybe.)

Like that hyphen you arrow could be *samskara*.
The dangers of the homalographic page as space
(could've been spice)
is that it might exclude the body
(The doctor puts needles in my back
and says I need to be faithful.)

Just think of the blur as flux, flax, bran.
You know, words
as white rice
not as good for you
as brown.

•

home-truths pin-apples part fossil through fertilization flight
or eyesight could be sky or ducks fishing

•

recognize the plumes   of a Spanish   kind   of writing
ancestors   as certain types of Atlantic
animals   something from Anatolia   with an "im" !

•

History of the sky engenders the diverse faces of religion
All kinds of stuff like hooks and coathangers inflate and
imprint there

                        Trace

                        (d)

•

War on your back
Raw no-words ruin
Real Clear Nuclear

•

"Ever try to copy Texas?
All those beans, all that plastic?"

— "I can hardly keep the road plowed."

•

HERE WE EVENTUALLY THERE EVEN VELOCITY A TIDE SUN
(SQUINTING) CIPED PAST THE ART THE SURREALISM OREGON JUST
HELP YOURSELF CLEANUP EGYPT AS A PLACE IN BRAZIL BUT NO
FURTHER EAST TIME AND RICE SEPTEMBER BURNT TEST TEST

•

thoughts different
sky's all animals, all
paper, all chalk. Our

•

writing as   the tableaus
anamorphous   =   of voyage
river cliffs   forgetting

•

            She danced the strict linguistic sense.
        babbled bavardage   finger-painted thick
            memo-clouds in the darkening sky

•

        h$_{om}$^{om}e

•

That's the secret
                    ticket
                            to silence
na [frame] na's notation

•

...each box of art jangles (peut-être)
a purchase on the edge of its own sequence
reflects adjacent body-language events even foreign
the container of white we unfortunately call history.

•

ohh   at nigh   night
Egypt
eh^x_____apⁱs_____apex

•

Maybe it was a dream grammar mountaining out the
hypostatic river as an approximate desire but instead
stretched striding or what I count on under the cedar tree
down by the road for final blue prints to the heart's property.

•

cellular memory linked to sunset effect
so *sunyata* revealed as absolute closure

•

I want one ethnic thing here,
right from the start. Dis-
orientation.

•

January birds
huddle on top of chimney
Wind the letter "A"

•

Loki, you
stomach

my sound.

•

Whenever I smell the raiments of message or caprice on you
I get jealous and reinvent old dance asterisks without code*.

*echoes

•

All the city
song, the great
city air.

Re a deer led to the lake only that fact self-conscious dare who say it again foraging for information behind this hotel we don't think anything of it but re membering that sometimes passes passion avec the memory of the very night songs played dromenon with life's loves perhaps even re collection as if that solved the wife and car syndrome collated at some later point like in the bank or bag pre played and reacted then drifted like continental tectons across at most three or four generations to make family re moon re sun settled self hunger honey just dessert.

ONE. What if the phemic blasted page so what was once transparent appeared an eye-spot burning paper you know with the sun and a magnifying glass erasing words instead of antheming another spiritual mirage imaged fate as predictable as a butterfly's flight plan.

TWO. A scent of the fall sheer memory snow smells meltdown this Everest morph more aperiodic than withershins and less likely resentment unioned by belief as a series of words than in the middle of juncture not standing like dawn hammers over the Himalayas but a flap-and-squawk V-line of geese.

THREE. If you could acquire a migrant invisibility in exchange for, say, sixty seconds, and that minute earth's contents recover moulting capability as well as faded anger with the presto of amoebean verses then walking forever instead of getting it back for nothing might turn the whiteout to remuda and you'd at least have hooves for tracks.

FOUR. Paratasein choice cut pickled and un knowing gravel to be one of the conditions of such motion slipp/ed from the pleasing though numbing eutaxia-tatooed sameness instead of.

FIVE. Is this an attempt to crack spin or a catalytic sugar made up to cotton the sweet uses of adversity with story's "then" planted in those spaces instead of poetry's timed gaze pivoted on possibility as opposed to prose's loss and what is measure pointing at if not that quaquaversal heat mountained up and spooned as dancing.

SIX. The sign of the turn plowed back into place as this world wheel scoops out preaction in a twinkle circumcizes heart such typhoon has no seersucker no milk no sugar.

SEVEN. If this renovation of memory turns out to be dérimage and we have to steer for the new world yet again in an elenxis of substitution then what now when the serial is only cinema and lists are needed before any action other than fishing which is best when it just *is* and not *for* anything.

EIGHT. Authority without text an illusion to master the distant and dissolving perimeter without search or government escaped containerism offers the tyranny of hot stuff contraband and never conquered without the fix or need for *dromenon* without the hook.

NINE. What drew river to share earth neither overtaking word was old scratch upon the world root radical that makes us taste like licorice unless you're white try ginger.

TEN. One reason why decimal was spotted on both sides of the centum/satam line was like the falling angel concurrently sighted with the same combination or polarity of surrender to the hieros except for the bird clouds interception of those tattooed letters rising from the city and maybe even this kind of patching of the rag.

ELEVEN. So there's this straight line to the question of hunger no way around the correct posturing of rule or guide me o righteousness not to answer but middle voice clot plugged with love-stutter simply wide need.

TWELVE. At first anguish sqeezed news out of a hostile terminology for red yellow black and brown but pretty soon languages become mouths of painful non-tint jargon poking into the dream and then all of a sudden with snare-drum crackling that heave of gut and protest untumbles the lock and *kapow!*

THIRTEEN. Sans souci the tongue hunts description until each morpheme gains kinaesthesis and then sharp motion pictures the memorable rousing as smoke or at least poked colour when smoked red.

FOURTEEN. Scope out the paragrams ahead and see if the divine isn't inhabited by some once-upon-a-time intention negotiable by a *shh shh* creeping up on curiosity as a kind of campground lure or kick the can espionage chance-cast into the emic abacus crying alley alley home free or any other text-spect (in-spect, re-spect, ex-pect).

FIFTEEN. After a while opinion becomes fierce burning and no longer dream has itself straight on how far from the cedar home is nor could nothing come in pieces even though tainted such dexterity in the world tree's branches takes hold and all you can do is shake violently these little boxes for books.

SIXTEEN. At least precious peace and the Friday saphire are still pupa'd into the sanctuary of message where anima equals the last bark of joy.

The distinct noise clarity makes from uncondemned memory beginning with small sheets of words turning very, very slowly slowing and knotting complete thoughts as sentences or fat stray objects probably stories of writing's reality dogs safely locked in waste land that far away from the perfect just goes to show what writers take for instance Bowering sans ing hopes for in a reader (confess it) mesmerized biotext not history not space but fear runs weeping from the imprint of fiction as a loaf of Triestian bread and all sorts of alibis for making sense right.

I've always had trouble with the ingenious engine as a suffix of graded wanting love or prayer especially kindergarten stifled kid as a kind of person who might extend racism or even keep me off the block your kindred jammed the oceans cognitive shot freeborn got then similar to most of the inborn tutelary spirits everywhere naive seed of Enyallion or old chip off the old rock and that's congenital heart buds gyna gendered and warped up tighter than a Persian rug how ginger's almost nicer than being born but that's just taste.

On the weekend I got into anger talk about
landscape and the hunger of narrative to eat answer or
time but space works for me because place got to be
more spiritual at least last felt now this watery genetic I
suspect passions like anger suprafixed to simply dwells I
mean contained as we speak of it believe me I'd like to
find a new word-track for feeling but language and
moment work out simply as simultaneous occurences so I
don't think you should blame words for time-lapse
tropism eg ethics is probably something that surrounds
you like your house it's where you live.

Again only is it in the thing itself the place which is
the driven place as a warm motor song hums under the
chakra tree rock or stone creek song I've become used to
such a thing always drowning and then owning myself
come to my own again possessed of me as the sib in the
place of itself hungry with love again forgiven dreaming
and knowing again the tailbone of itself bones claimed
again so that "thing" to my soul's bark floats again.

Don't do anything
just sit still and feel the bridge above
forget about the traffic
    it's going as fast as it can
down here is the river property
       no train of words except some tropic text of
truth about old creek song flows its utter pure of
coolness underneath the fading rose another rose
untangled knot a permafrost of frozen words
unflavoured dirt for roots
       all this leveraging aggregate compassed
grounding cord to compost loops the stomach's
locomotor to Gaian feedback shutdown more to
do with stellar steering of the junction box genetic
or the fresh-water hoofprint of salmon salt

Any gravel road's ok by me or is that an ordering
intervention so long as it's not pure highway to the end of
the void without my story our narrative's just a bunch of
rotten windfalls under the apple tree of someone elses
eye a statistical cluster made up to cover up and that
stupid notion of a project as sticking it to everyone else
instead of girdling yourself to the entelecheic text
underfoot that dreamt you long ago

an earth doesn't add up to the only implicate map
ethnos is and

the new doesn't have to be the purity nation is at
least some Love pictographed without lexicon gets us to
the grannies grammar.

This is no mass synapse I'm after and I've known awhile now being lost is as simple as sitting on a log but the fumble jerked mystique clouds grabbing as the staked mistake or stacked and treasured garbage belongs familiar to a gardened world disturbed as heat

O soft anxiousness to be found again and again estranged but marvellous then enlived slope of scree and marmot whistle so that synchronous foreignicity rages in music I want to put into a region of the cadence before falling's recognized you know

where there's that disgraceful ensoulment Mao called swimming.

If he thinks it's a great privilege to fill halls and talk about his own little heart when the invisible trunk of the noetic is what's available on the other side of the wall and only intuition can kiss the pebbly surface of Easter's stone just as "it is not you who throw the dart when you throw it" then could we not have called for a parallel conspiration to play out the alphabet onto the red carpet of one's body through some *himma* of potency no such dream of stars shld floor us by the raw and sober daylight of a cloudy sky.

Repetition of the body as a means of carrying imprint. Flowers, for example, couldn't get there any other way.

Looking at the ends first. Or that the digital eight hems. Aways prefer a circle route.

If this is the edge of of, that's skating. If those words aren't full of an ankle then nobody'll read them.

Mountains. Absolute mountains.

One night when the moon was below the horizon the one who had travelled farthest drew a grid on the beach. Supper was over and she used fishbones to detail parts of a bird. These were labelled p, u, and m. The kids sat on a log labelled w. Some of us realized later that the moon had gone under the lake and what rose above the ridge later that night could have been larger and crisper.

Out of death.

Well, this summer it was limestone again. Acres of it. And that's exciting because you could meander aimlessly. Not quite; I mean a fragment seemingly a trail might reveal itself and then maybe not.

Ten years from now I plan to stoke up the brush pile in the morning. Some word will.

Something stuck w/ no *dromena* until pre-problema solved the program of "forward" somehow the world you needled me age with words for such complex ingings of place and person that vertical I-beam shot through the top of my head in the Mexican cafe in Bernalillo ? (o crisp and drunken mountain moonlit night) such pepper still not now never silted out yet digging to remember such world and any other familiar thing, eh.

MUSIC AT THE HEART OF THINKING NINETY-SEVEN
(for Bob Creeley)

A collection of pomace. Left over. Residue. Pome poem. Fruit, of looming back yard pear tree. Windowed lost love, seasoned symmetry of gaze. Words to hang onto, picked, plucked, pared, preserved. Or rain/frost-rotted brown on top of the camper.

Nest. Branch and sky for hair. Dream space where the eye-shaktra's rooted up prime before the mind's eye in growth rings fluttered flowered house of interlimb, mesh of mindingness, net work, nest work.

Some bright beam lights up behind the eyes, or through the greenery, truths of all sorts writing pang and time. Tall is as old is. That's a fact. Things to put a bite on, the bark. Getting to the char-core heart with word-worm tunnelling. Put an ear to.

Low roar of shakuhachi waves. Enki drumming on the cedar. Hammered words said beep bent forgotten all but the ever-resonating thud even the paper-clean dry seed-head split and distant sound of frost released from brittle memory pod.

Old dogs of war words let loose as forkt birds slipping the private magic state into talking tree. Listen. Love words. Language paired and othered over the geographical heap, dangled from a canopy called earth-as-sky. Caw. Coo.

Facing the old yin-yang turbine round the night sky weaving its stars into the tree tops shade upon shadow questioning distance upon distant sites sign voice weather noting exed ever only spins plus minus minus minima plus.

After the throttle cutting of white inked into body along with the sigh of staining the world with the same body. What a river such tangible surfaces usher singing; its banks cut too with smells and other signs of shape or touch tuned with Meloids.

Word as seed preserve brings up the notion of rotten language composting for the progeneration of itself and the ripe vocable as soft and juicy palpable but for the bite of belief and the Bering Isthmus migration so far from the Cantonese pollen.

Chinatown walking through the food smelling and then sitting down in a booth to taste the birds-nest soup or any noodle late night neon ragtime all alone in the dawn music Virgil's vigil down the street and home again home again.

Stirred-up word leaves equal to birds' startled whoosh and the morphophonic fruiting of the great vowel shift(s) syllable canting the old prayer wheel so familiar as the resonating fat of the adjective, you know, like "Summertime."

The tropisim of allowing the range of stimulation (in this case, sky) and avoiding such an indicator as clarity of outline (that is, fingering it) puts the poet's nose to the wind so that bite has surface (in fall, that could mean frost).

Yes, there are a few of those brushes with sudden silence. The "great" hush. A slight stunning of the uttering tongue diverts to rainforest and you know OM is AM somewhere on the hermes dial. Even the trees wait, rooted.

Here the wickerwork of wonder prevails, especially seasonally, especially winter. Night turns too. That's when the griddle glows with answers, that's when the porch of stars or clouds twigs to the forecast, that's when the eyes get used to the dark.

This stoniness that comes to life, unfetters itself from heap by song and the crazy clicking of the compass needle from side to side, something ringing ahead, something diamond, vertebraeic, maybe something bonelike in the name.

Sometimes it's just word as a reflective buoy nunning and canning entrance to the (h)arbour. At others, smell's left to gauge place, especially in the morning. The ode as a jar for dead fingernails. Pears, breathing through their skin.

Here's the tree traveller with news from the roots. For the poet that's the "heavenly" one, the one growing down from above. Not just dream. The tune is reflective: the image of the tree shows a tree. Such is home and the authority of love.

The tree-talk hears preaction (ie, just thinking about it) as a plot to rejuvenate the locomotor birth-breath effect (you know, when the sap rises) because there always seems to be an un- or de- chat to simulate houseness.

Layered into west-coast leafery is another homing device between the legs for birds, rivers, salmon, spawning gravel, and smouldering midden heaps. All old time warm, damp copulas charting ocean's peaks to get some home again.

Mother tongue tied lost ungendered gendering potent cone-seed to burst birth in any chance fire only words green branching into childhood pink Eve's apple stuck in man's throat all forest foreign but for the pear tree.

Behind this tree-braille on the slivered moon-pear of a page is his "screech" and behind that some solitary hollering of the pome poem as proper, as in *proprio*, vessel for any world-preserved jar of memory keeps listening for.

Tell-tale leaf-light filtered photosynthetic compost haunted by the house syntax. Paper page so under the thinking thumb, but then the word baggage tsunamis forth and tosses, say, the persona of language's song which then just dangles and spins.

Ancientness moving in on the dream of falling. Air drama, into the earth. Leaf-word-paper-skin-mould, moist churnowing of a tongue once flowered container of the "well" sprung within body sapling dappled skylight seeded.

"s" love and South America not yet past her (larger now) foot,
bone, beak, star
beyond CBC oral — Swoop Safeway
          nebulae threw notions of panic this is — Cool
spring Paris
that's the wind through one of those piazzas
immigrate land knows sense the stick said water
                              could turn
to snow — Exo/ekto
what's the dif since memory meant to carry over flake.

What I wants is a western Miss Am — Fascinated
by the spelling of Erika
left out of the deck work
rail watching out for the lean — Just like that
eye danced edge can smoke "the"
                    avec some ing.

Some poems name song and dream as an instrument with
which to pass by — Always a little distance calling over the
snow behind the trees to please observe the camerals.

Much white within bird.
North in August, that's their fall.

Light bends nice, in the mountains folds
each hill tucks late day.

Breath is the bridge all along, a winter sign.
Tongue's frozen words, air.

Then sigh said it again
remembered something.

Only the news hand tapped out of
shoulder a single white feather.

Text still as the lake this evening cantoed time late history birded into the space nest the really real or as they say now in Banff the virtual line gone fishing.

Song as wood chiming way past the rim shot further even than any one instance of drumming and always outside the sign parade even Jupiter aligns with Sunday school before singing Star of.

Being led by words isn't so bad at least you can count on them or they're like counting every time pebble registers clear then there's the next leaf or ferry and if the distance of the world doesn't work ignore the busy signal and dial syllable AM herst 6-5740 talk about being led by the news.

Some plumed finger hot for some sun drawn into thicket paradise's bird of Reaching vision lands too close for binoculars and suddenly years of cadence suck the manufacture of duration into the middle distant voice so there you see for you yourself.

MUSIC AT THE HEART OF THINKING ONE HUNDRED AND ONE

Line is a cut point to point
half of one world the other half
still available.

Anything but the next word
hold the present moment for as long as
you can hold your breath.

Anchors away with a sigh or me
caught with a double you too always fishing
at the bottom of the bookshelf.

Heard enough of industrial hearts somebody
called him hammerhead and I thought
he'll never learn grammar.

Book stripped tree to logos stump some
lumber caught scale and went to jail that truck of
interstellar logging events.

If they stacked us by our first names
we'd be at eye level Phyllis Fishstar half
truth at the Shinto Gate.

On one side sigh hangs and through a window sand and flowering vetch land's a floater or some simple blunt of weight against balance just another frozen pea-bag to shoulder mind at un poco, un poco a turtle measure of memory proprio'd slightly above and two feet behind your mouth moving to intercept the note intended as Loki's cue to lift song no repetitious paper dragon chinatown or any city for self this rhetor caught in our maws had better be shaken or the Tienanmen.

1

Some body parts of the move into the world
show up as replacement parts
Is there a finger or is there a tongue
to be recognized later
perhaps Is like walking
cameraed through the European woods
and peripheralled out to Paris *bois* by bus on Sundays
lean gap as if creek stone or hand over mouth
how do we watch for logs and other dendrita
there curled (check weather report)
layered along the banks so that part flows/makes sense

2

Fiction's window for example
my neighbor and the prairie sun shifted
single ridge-pole into two tip-to-butt cedars
who now knows what news when she opens the roof
closer to paradise and strapped to her door each
morning
such fashion for today tests for sky's emptiness the
figment
and dance of any (finger) pigeonhole aperture

3

Tree the word
becomes eye-pegged business *virtu*
all Jack O'Lantern realism just a piece of cheese cake
snap to lock title page careens out of tilt
or should if the virago would just cry out the curious
but doesn't this plastic sign need (doesn't need)
either tight gut silence or stony story

4

To evanesce is possible
in just over two thousand feet
such separations today silk our covers to touch
just to mull over the marred surface of thought
glazed with snow — silhouette visible
no need to look up even breathe

5

Who told stomach how
as if to depend on sigh signing
enough to blight the plan-hole
now just try this one out okay
walk in on the true dark
that same blue
no catastrophe but only so many nights ever

6

Straight 4/4 time but just a little
clouded over the ridges
just a little eye in the sky little riff for the skiff
even what gaze set off toward first rock
until hackled in white somehow 'istory
all our farm clocks telling
get that package to the edge of the river
where it waits for the pickup while out on the bridge
how does the page gel root at the same time how does
the double tongue ripple the noon day pond

7

An assumed name and voice thinking
hum can look so scared shitless with edges

is that a problem the north follows around
meanwhile period
pencil finger thumb rubbers the 'story of the book
and post-place
is that the point or dipper of the American drum
or is that coke

8

A quick blink
but just because the first page turned quiet
doesn't mean we'll forget
in fact nothing cellular about time
the supper bell'll ring
whenever belling's needed

9

Sometimes leaning shows
but after that architecture churches
a picture of the perfect ridgepole as a nautilus transit
mere yawing on the backside of the planet
saved as virtual in the promise of belief
only one before belief two
then how did she know it was all
tight ripple-grain around the knot now a ladder

10

No secret tidal
dialogue moving in
on the almost
open Persian Gulf
from under such

cradled rhythms
anima hemmed in
by all eight mountains
counting

11
Being born grammatically correct
isn't technically season
just wordless options for genre
until good luck's red paper's peeled greeting
severed scrap sewage new year's
year of the yet named
time starts tale varooming page
to spine page to spin

12
gut cut
but touch
still stirs
slight all-American gung
straight-arrow sign
language plays
in the cards

13
Unthawed tongue
talk talk talk
telling the wind names
found in foreign currents
the sound of quivering rudder
biblio'd at the heels
but just local
locally twisted

14

Then what kind of pattern can you back
into when lake and river surface eclipse in
that diagonal sparrow of global day-to-night
which becomes then the other story
known as the Norwegian surface until
someone from inside Quebec quizzes how
deep's the paper in that official manner
meant to determine bona fide spic-and-
span krino-sift

15

How to get the lyric to emerge
where the paraph boils
is that the purpose
of the combing process volte-face
of a tripartite world's stiff calibration
of enlisted tactics to get home or even around town
but to arrive at the stem of a new world all portrait
or how else undice the lustre of the line

16

From late afternoon almost to dusk by the
time they get maybe seven nibbles at
America and then

Art formatting rosy-fingered paradise when
who else but animus tries on the
Massachusetts slaver forgetting that the
hook was baited in favour of hunger even
though they've practiced can you tell the
chubby cooks their reputation's not left
untouched

17

Is it really because the moon was tied to the pilings
with maybe five or six gamblers suggesting the next move
just because the lake we live on is a dog-leg lake
or did she strike out within ear-shot of the tin drum
chimes hazarding what old cliché on virtue
from the glossary of voices in novels and valleys basket
if so
then how can we believe the fiction of trips
will deter the determined nextness of story

18

What good is it
if her ears heard gut
how lucky his rabbit
didn't doubt eyes
like periwinkle knives
or the binnacle housed rowboats
(and that was Belief One)
from earlier days deep
into the night

Noah couldn't think in words
except to mutter grammar plus,
that asphalt tongue had to be a tenor
so what good is it to involve artifice
just to come up with something

19

Certainly up around Leduc
Alberta pressure-treated virgin duck
there before pure bush-whacking made maps literal

gills is what gets us up the hill of the genitive
appendix but breeched birth's anger no euphoria
no end of any story gingerly born
just more sons who can work
the final name shift but each daughter stuck
with a tongue to taste the frozen rail

20

Some granite over her shoulder
into the wind, Toronto
balmy, almost sun through the haze.

This is her mediterranean eye:
crushed stone cement lamp-posts
stained with rust from the bolts.

Sneaks a quick flash of wood at home
determined to double her mirror

21

What annex of names for northern Europe
not calendered
under a tripod of blackened driftwood
totemed upright on the beach
could gutteral the night without blur
and craving infiltration charcoal gone
wild for alibi

22

Is this ladder to decline the yoni
or to invert the horns of the ziggurat
to the clit of desiring night.

Whatever kind names
jazz at the Palladium,
same cross. No noodles.
Just steam our fish in black bean sauce
and something bitter.
Or why the main character
has a nose to job.

23
How if why pirate the genre ship
when you can try stamping the body
with the flood of forty-eight
back then it was no secret
we would all share the same formula
for invisibility intended to clock (snow.)
(quells.) (sameness.) (time.)
and time again

24
To say says mouth
words story spicy news
or ciping the Green Door
for Shanghai noodles
she says they said pretend
but snuff with Hermes' stealth
no need to filter the action
why not atmosphere this form tonight
right under your nose
back into the menu

25

At the Wildlife Centre is a "Turtle Crossing" sign

that the body story follows earth

that's what we could learn then

what the wall of sensation nurses

to avoid but revere the key

and then what the hand seeds,

all cards to guide the next bluff romance

26

Shouldn't we begin with the sort out and deliver task

since that sets the pulse

and whatever the Sirs say

don't stop at the border to mime fragment

every true esthetic rifles her lied on Saturdays

those're those purple afternoons

27

Some of these feathers washed up

draw out the local what.

Could that be science's sack of the positive?

So stomp!

28

You can have a side-to-side door

a side door

a door that opens and closes

and if you want a door that disappears

then you'll get a real name allergy

but if you get tired of the code of theory

especially those cute rectified arts like the novel

plus the one that goes up and down
the one with stomach cramps

29

What comes with all that temporal morphology
that endless propagation of the sub-father
that belt the son is left to shine
no sharp, no axe needed
for re-reading the rough opening
and now will animalism handle that hatch
to blaze our spin right outa there

30

Isn't how she could plan keeping
dependant on Plato's spread
if the transitive purposing plot
comes all the way around
to repeat the solar stamp
you know, gets too singular
and repetitive almost platelike
these charts of government

31

Maybe we could strip
this ponderous ark of size
and sniff page
right into the gutter
with the numbers
seeing as how humming's
flood's filled
no wash no meaning
but very clean no punctuation

32

nine

nin

nie

the three *belle-lettres*

33

No clear-cut logging on this property

if you think of the margin as a wing

how would you not contain story

or think of a menu of alignment

accidenting itself on the driver's side

34

No

not a sigh in site

nor could "ı" find

design in singing

35

Housing always knows

we find out even

when we only understand

the lie

if above the clysmic bark heaves
noise the voice detonates images and
words for life a little crazy we
think but all right before the actual
figures choose choice the border
labels space in you

if any persistent tissue bristles pitapat
on the heart's much too excited lip
could be the air's too rare
naturally some same body
remembers too late
to search for another wave

if a small cup of language
soups intention with a continued
expression against word crust
until the horizon of approach
whose fault whose lips

if the forest of the voice
transforms into the trop of chaos
or melancholy installs itself
in the parlour of surprise plant
variety re-speak pond

if the see-saw bounces back hot to trot
trembling shows up again late cell
synapse applied part out on
a day of rest great truth
a vague smack of the lips
gulfs, coral, littoral

if, you tremble, you should see
inevitably there is some white
it is true and of course
you tremble

MUSIC AT THE HEART OF THINKING ONE OH FIVE
(IF YES SEISMAL, from "Si sismal" in à tout regard by
Nicole Brossard)

Take anything Max Ernst you fish as much as the birds eyes horses so the eyes are the same the eyes are not always the same look right into the wood like heart right? say through plaster-cast dactyllic to feel in a knot eyes and in the wood eyes out of the wood or a figure cut from Un Chinois Egare A Lost (Bewildered) Chinaman he called it natural history you can imagine the silk print since youth stare at things at any things.

encaustic "you"
literal vertical history
making french factory garments
your painting called "Slate"
imagine time made up
of materials besides "wood, various
papers, pins, powder
pigment, felt
pen, graphite,
india ink, mask-
ing tape,
plexiglass"

I believe you

but to not know thinking
whatever you called it
is never impossible so
the contemporary past "information"
so necessary to use stuff and other
wonder about it then
never name it, Irene

Yet another picture of tree I think opened up forests of thought or trees maybe by washed out glaze simply making outline eyes half closed remembering some truth tree made up of many nor not sure colour could do it water underneath all surfaces enlarged touched hut of my mind literal no-name watercolour simple yet suggested and entered old fallen tamarack Helen limb peeling itself back into same earth.

the Idea, Henri
moves

"Mouvements 1950" in sumi sign
tachism repeats

seeing
saying

appearances and agitations
not just the rock surfaces
mind, too, splashes
expression all over

that mescal uneasiness
quivers

why you studied medicine
yet became a sailor
suddenly 1922 "art"
and February '83
into the Seibu in Ikebukuro

they know, they know
you have a hint of something
dirt
at the surface you thought
to whisper
a little gossip

in words "these
amazing and subtle...
pigments

of the period
>you walk on the stones of the earth
>each day of your life
>stone after stone

>water will not match
>>this painted tissue or stainless steel

>"Saera
>Conversazione"

you know, regarding blush

and Pudeur

rouge pad, our mother's

all woman, Indiana's "Year
of Meteors 1961" earlier

forget to sing, forget the song
(Chatham: Blue Yellow)
>I have to know   all of this, like this
these
>subtle
talk song talk sign
>(ta dum)

The Hands

tres petit
but vociferous

layers and layers lies
noises born in Canada

trees w/ meaning tight
French sentences, played w/

number
a clarinet, a glass of sherry

they yell meaninglessly Phyllis
this birdlike looking, looking

O Frank Stella so inscribed the light symmetry on dark terrific revolving really painlessly the sun in New Lo Angeles Israel then interesting some stand (set) free of less than that than that the script sure of the surface especially Jill 1959.

Jennifer whoever
in the garden, nautical
post-reflection

under water person
or her daughters
embryo of typograph/glyph

shows the idea eyesight builds up
and with light
from the surface

         material

(dirt)
substance projection mathematical almost carried

via optical mixture
(points) on white on white

but you do that in a garden
that's what you do
you plant

At Sea

so green the red, John, border
w/ words, "the" words
                    AT SEA
the water a green somewhere
suggests your blues
as in crayons, the World
Wieners by Ron Kitaj
Leatherstocking on the wall of the Kyoto British Council
"Lapis Lazuli," light food up the dark alleyway
1966, 1938. Steaming. Steering.

from the ceiling
full of "heart," Nana

why not
sneeze again Duchamp

in 1954 my father's car
coming and going

I remember phanopoeia's casting
getting into Jon Whyte's Banff

when you are 26 your
"Trees" are everything

"Bagatelle for Albers"
"Pennies from Heaven"!

no not colour
leading out along the road late to catch the last ferry
maybe the eyes (smoke) hint

(pink
and the shapes slippers
Jed August
moon
Kate

Jack Wise/Christopher Smart and
psycho-
       holograms
Giuseppe Tutti (is that
right?)

Whole earth all over
problem site sand
Blake going for no frame
full bleed

Marian Dennis Running Arms
Susan Penner Curly Hair
Baldlike Sleigh Machine
Pyramid Wheeler Outstretched Seattle

Moon

flight crayon pink plywood backing
for christmas une guerre civile 1971
memory embraces on the lawn chair
her legs (Susans?) disappear 1977 1987
whistling

Are those your rusted rocks along our shore?

Those lifelike mammals shallowed long

and flaunting in green water

lolling bellies that fish fish-shine

pure lapping thought smoothed out

sailors-take-warning morning?

Yet at that time of day flight becomes bothersome

since these are the returned over not so much land

nor arctic eyes

but the shining piss

of the philosopher's stone

noctiluca

glowed last night, soft

just like the moss.

Mailbox + Letters Winter
Words + Terrace Out Tree mount No.3 that
plus QNNET no meshwork, Domain
and Message Router Myfile {to} friend

the info texted invisible
lofts afloat w/ masks
and image of the year as measure
'd logged out
bit scaped
more than just another marked ear framed

Try seeing some March 4
quelques de fabric

life and love (marriage)
her dress maybe

199 Lyndal Drive
                Dear Dave

it could be some kind of affixation
no joke but blueprint

even Toronto as an event
can get like that at five.

Spots of blue dripping the "s" as a ship or at least underwater and that not-so-little entrail of green like a ranch boxed in fields of white blizzards square problems in an active flux.

Or that "s" as some other kind of anchor outside this fuss.

Like that.

That little charcoal field up north and the ACE 1962 R.Kitaj not.

from Schwitters' "Und" no political or social meaning

knot or note for Nietzsche's Gay Scientist

Dreaming from Magritte's "The Reckless Sleeper" 1927

some mind-work as a mirror

Egypt actually discovered that birdlike symmetry

(but for the "т" over her head)

and then pawprint loses out to glassiness (apples)

tree

Blake's room along w/ Samuel Palmer's "visions

and models of the exquisitest pitch of intense poetry"

pitch,

    and dim light

    the morning stars

(Jane Shore's penance)

      "equal   paradise

      in all essential points"   keeps

                             kindled

Ahead art envelopes Beuys's 4 Blackboards while included
in the width cubism narrated signage his word for it
"economics" arrows for HAPPINESS lazy reread

to shine fate determining futurism while a will selects
dance

and away far away.

What with the air or brick and you open wide in the blue intense blue sweater electro-magnetic field coordinates of the entire swoop run north/south tumblers interlocked at the code post-elastic in case anybody gets to you about your cheeks sit in that blue waiting all over the background your mind world beyond the wall even the dress you wear mapped Dutch desire.

ARTKNOT TWENTY-ONE

The happy lady and the bird 1949 or maybe some boomerang of a dark blue moon's always been life with chalk Joan's muttered words on the sidewalk scotched plan fresh game ahead hop slope and tree the flyball inside old catalogue mitt such sign as stone thrown to box fetter counting with wishes on sky dome.

Nash's silent wood quarry diagrams lexicon of tree
spread bucked and split limbed sawn debarked and
quartered burnt piled dadoed spliced peeled screwed
nailed kiln-dried then baked bent laminated skidded
thrown tripped hugged buried finally old cedar tree felled
in gulley voiced in thimbleberry no dream no bear.

ARTKNOT TWENTY-THREE

So sad 1920 Beckman carnival
could've magnetized this place
this page cld.

Matisse yr such a disappointment today yr esprit humain cannot save the boredom of a lifetime of nude prints money and beauty even both banks like the jazz that comes out of the mouth or yr flower letter to André Rouveyre otherwise who cld believe now those're yr clichés'd prefigured Paris.

Jean and Jean Crotti and Degottex.
So what about the arrow "Explicatif...?"
and writing "time" by head and hand
but never behind with feathers or dreaming
as the sign art things touch it it's
just a fingerprint?

Schumann frequencies the earth
our hearts harmonize seven
point eight per second
the neuron horizon

circles the lake-nests
Osprey gone, the burning season
hub of pilings, hub of water
the day hue fades, buzzes

to stop fish this port closed
still shudder but lap lap bough hanged
summer
bark

February sun hot car melting radio from see bee sea ekphrastic stilling in the damp headliner air with the windows rolled down to parity as a go between Hank Bull's AM art echoes Bob and Ray wishing "you folks in radioland could see these photographs" phantopoeic ventriloquist hum through the poplar branches snow giving way to Gombrich's Apatropaic image just some wood chipped away, feet to a table, claws, just above the dashboard, waves.

Cracked surface times that the lake or sea bed walked edge and
    the path made reflective

stone

outside of romance let's embroider our mirror right to the true
    optopotent body

Christine's holy city coned

Hyperbole's moving bull's-eye

plane

reflection

echo

projection

cave

film

gauze

scat

entrail

residue

page

leaf

pile

book

descent

ocean

gaze

reprint

track

screen

tulle

actual

emergency of maps
shape of puddles
fruit of words
pith of whales

that threads In   S fold:
D facto   you mythic yet:
her M   more   red fire:
next K   than 'membered S1:
line S2 y9ou F edge.

Outside Emily Carr's lone piss-fir these throats that
are long in art and free-standing poems wall the provinces
no more rail yelling every spike a chink.

ARTKNOT THIRTY-THREE

Glenbow's sensation of the body femin
ism made for thirst

some guy's art wire heart
post-marble still thinking nature/natural

uptitled I was made for having
lapped "at" her tears